LAND OF AMNESIA

LAND OF AMNESIA

Poetry

Joseph Bathanti

Press 53
Winston-Salem, NC

Press 53
PO Box 30314
Winston-Salem, NC 27130

First Edition

Cover design by Kevin Watson

Cover photo by Joseph Bathanti

Author photo (p.83) by Jan Hensley

Printed on acid-free paper

ISBN 978-0-9816280-7-3

For Joan,
"my best beloved"

Acknowledgments

Many thanks to the editors of the following publications in which these poems originally appeared, in some cases slightly different versions: "Drought" in *Aethlon*; "Design" and "Wall at Second Manassas" in *Appalachian Heritage*; "The Vilas Flood" in *Appalachian Journal*; "Epigenesis" in *Asheville Poetry Review*; "The Christian Ventriloquist" in *Barrow Street*; "Holy Week" in *Chattahoochee Review*; "First Christmas Eve, Charlotte 1977" in *The Charlotte Observer*; "John" in *Cumberland Poetry Review*; "Something from a Book" in *The Hollins Critic*; "Advising" in *Iodine Poetry Review*; "Madonna" in *Iris: The UNC Journal of Medicine, Literature and Visual Art*; "Joan of the White Car" in *Mount Olive Review*; "Land of Amnesia," "The Note," "Rendition," "The Haybaler," "Forgotten County," and "Running" in *NC Crossroads*; "House-Hunting at Four Thousand Feet" in *Literary Trails of the North Carolina Mountains*; "How to Bury a Dog," "Pumpkins," and "The Spirit Homeless" in *North Dakota Quarterly*; "Bath" in *Outer Banks Magazine*; "The Christian Ventriloquist" in *The Owen Wister Review*; "Deer Catacombs" in *Passages North*; "White Lake, Bladen County" in *Pembroke Magazine*; "Off South Carolina 9 in Little Rock" in *Poem*; "The Immaculate Conception" in *The Recorder*; "Peaches" in *The South Carolina Review*; "Black Vulture" and "Julian" in *Sow's Ear Poetry Review*; "The Cartographer" in *Weber Studies*.

"The Stonecarver," exactly as it appears in this volume, hangs, as a dedicatory poem, in The Statesville (NC) Train Depot. A much shorter and vastly altered version of the poem has been performed and recorded by The Cockman Family.

"Land of Amnesia," "The Note," "Rendition," "The Haybaler," "Forgotten County," and "Running" won the 2002 Linda Flowers Prize, awarded annually by the North Carolina Humanities Council.

Also by Joseph Bathanti

Poetry:

Communion Partners
Anson County
The Feast of All Saints
This Metal

Novels:

East Liberty
Coventry

Short Stories:

The High Heart

Nonfiction:

They Changed the State: The Legacy of North Carolina's
Visiting Artists, 1971-1995

Contents

I.

Tell all the Truth but tell it slant—
Success in Circuit lies

—Emily Dickinson (1129)

Land of Amnesia

I swear, given even this much
of a fool's chance, at the end
I'd beg to cross one last time
the Rocky River into Anson County.

I'd ask you to come;
and if you'd so consent,
I'd foreswear tobacco and shun drink.
But the bill of sale

this time would be forever.
No last minute dickering over the route,
no trips to the conjure woman
like Lot's lying wife.

I'll not have you looking back.
We'll hold Jesus to his writ
promise of forgiveness—
not in such tongue as folks might reckon,

but signs, bodement:
two nights of bloody sun
over All Souls Church,
shades in the vesture of deer,

your hand in mine atop Lord Anson's Bible.
Over Cedar Hill and Pinkston
we'll shin the tar roads and foxtrots,
critter-quit but for snakes in oatgrass.

Even a mincing moon off cotton will yield
light enough to walk by.
In the morning I'll be there
with sweet milk. We'll watch the sun

break out of the crop-shroud
like a borning baby, lustering the brake,
wild banshee turkeys sailing out of it.
If we make Brownie's trailer by lunch,

he'll put us up something:
field peas and hoecakes, blueberry honey.
From His firmament the Lord will fix us
in the cross-hairs of His holy roads,

109 and 1634,
Big Davis on the shoulder,
black as old roadbed,
hitching into Wadesboro

for a jug of wine at the shothouse;
a game of nine-ball clacking
out the open door of Deese's speakeasy,
two mulecarts and a pickup with a tethered

Bluetick chocked in the gravel.
From here,
it's not but a mile and half to the infallen
arsoned house, where we first whelped.

But you are bound to be frighted.
It gets fen and swampy.
River runs under this murmurry ground.
You can smell the charred heart-pine,

turpentine what boiled out in the fire, pitch
so fast and instant bird-flocks that lit there
singing still roost by their petrified bones.
Nailed across the door is a whiffletree.

Mrs. Little's thorns still thrive.
The old bay, Star, dead two decades,
canters in the pasture.
Cotton fetches two bits a bale.

In the sky dart lights of other craft.
There's no one we can tell about this,
no one who would ever allow it.
Behind us pitches the crazed compass needle,

our lives of other counties long forgotten,
burnt up like hair-locks in a candle.
It is here, my best beloved,
we'll build on ruin.

Running A Group Home

Someone had shot our dog.
The photographs of my wife at the time
show her gaunt and papery,
attempting to pay attention,
but drifting off as if seeing
or hearing an intruder at the edge
of the cropped frame she peers from.
She's not clearly herself,
in some of them half-clothed.

Not even a year into our marriage—
the sheriff delivered the children to us
in the middle of the night.
They called us *mama* and *papa*.
We petted and kissed them
as if they were ours,
tucked them in with thrift
comforts and Teddy Bears,
and went ourselves upstairs to bed.

They'd come alive then.
Through the ductwork we'd hear
beer cans pishing open
and matches struck,
their little bodies
machining into one another,
the fever of their music turned low.
The smell of marijuana.

Small flashes of their whispered lives
sparked out of the heat vent,
illuminating our love-making
we tried like one-night standers
to conceal. In the morning
they'd be there to wash and feed
and take to school in the County van.

We'd stagger naked out of bed
and go to our only window,
look out over Roosevelt Boulevard.
On the other side was a dyeing
and finishing plant; then beyond it—
we could see its perimeter lights—
the Union County Prison Camp.

The dog, from the pallet
we had laid by our bed,
in his sleep whined
like a nightmaring convict
for his mother.

Joan of the White Car

*I am not so sure that I do not
sometimes mix up the historical Joan
with the legendary Joan. No matter.*
— "Joan of Arc—'Go Boldly'"
— Candida Lund

A brimstone girl turned bold
and beautiful, she lit candles
and, as described in her diary,

*stared into the blue-hooded flicker
until it became a burning teardrop
at the center of sight,*

*a vision, then
a voice persisting sainthood,*
urging her to ride

*the witch-burning backwater
charred with Klan crosses
like ampersands tallying*

the estate of terror.
On the Feast of All Souls, 1976,
after repeated *consort* with her

soul's namesake and patron,
she charged in her big white Fairlane
Venoble's Field, in the small

Georgia village where she was born,
*prilling it with tongues
to pale the Holy Ghost Himself,*

8

Wizards and Dragons fleeing their robes—
and was later arrested,
given over to churchmen

and tried for blasphemy.
No one greeted her,
though all the town marshaled—

vengeful, *uninformed by Archangels
and desire*—to witness
her cakewalk through clay

and cotton to the stake,
the *tarriance of flame*
in the folds of her red dress.

First Christmas Eve Together, Charlotte, 1977

There is one bulb out
on the widower's string of yule lights.
He lifts like a torch a clear glass quart
of Miller High Life and sings

Adeste Fidelis from his listing verandah
around which vagrants in thrift swaddling
gather, their mouths clenching
and unclenching, trying to fix onto

the words as one might the memory
of a blizzard playing over a town
trapped in a child's paperweight.
From our rental's hearth we sit watching

as they carol along the street, flames
sliding as if on black ice along the sterno log.
Our tree, cut from county right o'way,
wears modestly its twenty blinking lights,

foil star and package of blue balls
that round like funhouse mirrors
everything into something else.
Arbored into the bottom branches

is a hand-me-down creche:
a jacklegged shepherd propped against
the plump Christ-child's manger;
the kings abstracted; Joseph

and Mary worn, their gold plaster
nimbuses notched with age;
the cattle on their sides for want of hooves.
Jesus never had much.

From a few blocks away
a cantata of sirens, then
the pilgrims' tread on our porch floor.
We open the door and in they toddle,

muttering through their stubble a song
of joy and triumph, blessing us
in our ignorance. We take from the freezer
and offer them the saved top tier

of our wedding cake, bride and groom
smiling from their snowy yard.

Madonna

(After the photograph of her mother by Liz Priestly)

Like evidence the image slips
out of the white envelope

addressed to me, the subject
an ancient near naked woman in profile,

draped in mosquito bar.
She looks at once chrysalid and marble,

a statue of gnarled smoke
levitating against the oily black paper,

her oddly powerful legs slightly bent,
torso hunched forward, the head

with that chiseled, death-mask androgyny
of a Greek bust, fluted,

cottony hair, features of implacable, timeless nobility.
But her eyes, unlike those Thracian amnesiacs,

are not alabastered shut.
Rather the sockets chock wide

with the shutter-flash that turned her to stone.
In her lap, nearly invisible

for the roil of gauze,
she cradles what can only be a baby,

it too petrified,
the skull the size of a prehistoric egg,

little x-ray face like a soul effigy
carved into a tombstone.

Another World

(for Susan Cresswell)

There were things on earth I wanted shed of:
a certain future in West Tennessee, men,
twisters, Shiloh. I'd dress up:

loose shirtwaist, turquoise,
Chantilly, smoke a joint,
head in the truck for some hinter place

where they'd likely show:
farm roads, meadow churchyards.
They favored dusk.

I'd read up on it.
Hovercraft like rhinestone
pinwheels, the radio

fuzzing over and a sudden
cicada-muting wind
flattening June's brown wheat,

the air sizzling with chaff;
the soft metronomic *thunka-*
thunka; then a pulsing

ray like an Ed Wood movie.
I'd close my eyes. Have you ever been
in love with a liar, but didn't care?

Have you, clutching orange poppies,
ever levitated into the oncoming,
begging kindness from another world?

How to Bury a Dog

Put to bed the children early.
The moon refuses such toil.

Arcturus will stand you the proper light.
Fall to your knees.

Let your wife's hair grieve
your mouth as you hold her.

She'll swear she hates everything.
Don't say a word.

Choose a place among the loblollies
where the first sun burns

the cornflowers blue.
Take the long-handled shovel

and the garden spade,
the mattock and the maul.

A shotgun will do—12-gauge Federal—
for what you'll be digging in:

millstone grit studded with milk crystal quartz.
It will suffer your hands.

At grave-time, dirt is coy,
not a fit place to leave what you love.

You won't cuss through three feet
until you spark off a shelf

of sediment rock that's been making
since the Yadkin lived here.

Resist the temptation
to wrap him in cerements.

Face him east.
Let the earth do its work.

The Pear Tree

At the base of this tree
I sit
and read the poems

of Humberto Ak'abal
to my children.
A few white blossoms

with hearts of pink,
the shape of Guatemala,
still linger in the upper branches.

I should stop now.
I have written my own poem;
but next to the tree

is the stump of its brother.
I pick two of the hard tiny pears
and give them to the children.

The peasants call such fruit *indigena*,
local to this rocky soil.
They ripen and fall and just lay there.

I wish I could read
these poems in their native K'iche,
but they would be too terrible

for the little ones, munching
on their pears as if
they had stolen them,

terrible the way a mother
whose fatherless babies
are hungry is terrible—

not so much the hunger,
nor even the babies,
but the mother

and the rough grey hills
to which she must spirit them.
I look at the pear tree

and call out to it.
My eyes know it for a friend.
But it does not call back,

even when I drop the book
and my children and I
wrap our arms around it.

The Haybaler

Wandering an elbow of cotton, long-harvested,
straggled with soiled white swabs on spindles,
and limish-yellow, pollen-slick leaves
given over after a cold snowy spring

to heatspore. Blessed rot.
Raiment aplenty for the dying cropland.
Glittering work the harrow makes of quartz.
In its middle roots the rusted haybaler,

manufactured in St. Joseph, Missouri,
a Canadian patent stamped into it.
Four rungs lead to a platform, gibbet high,
a vertical conveyor chain,

withered locks of timothy
in its bloody broken teeth.
I can't help but think of Waite Trickham
at the White Store Café in Anson County

every day at noon dinner.
With his only hand removing
his banded straw hat,
setting it on the table,

then reaching with it for Mrs. Trickham's hand
to return thanks in bowed silence.
And she, mouth a slit,
cutting his meat,

lovely in that demure Southern suffering mien,
how sealed as if in paraffin was her heart
like a murdered saint's.
For half a century

she'd not been held with two arms.
Waite's hanging sleeve was stitched, I tell you,
as if each morning, like ablution,
she hemmed the stump into it.

He remained shy,
his face blunt, burnt clay.
That haybaler took his arm,
and still it takes it.

Takes it as the clouds slowly shift,
white flannel slipping from blue shoulders,
bare blue breasts a crow spraddles
like a boy's first crucifix.

Black Vulture

Arthritic stockings grey,
she limps about the corpses
on the cage floor.

The head too is grey,
carrion-colored,
blubbered at the wattle,

whittled to the beak.
We've made of her viduity
the likeness of a witch.

She senses our loathing,
hawks up something, coquettishly
circles it, keeps on us

an oracular eye, then unclasps
her shawl of feathers.
Between the trembling wings

gaunts the white-splotched breast.
Obedience lured her out of the sky,
love of cosmos, vow of silence,

sacrament. For the mystery
of body and blood is with her,
she that looks not away

at the transubstantiation, swallowing
the flesh with the soul still beating within;
there always, black angel,

at the instant of our deaths.
And we, host eaters of the dead,
look upon her with Christian dread.

Deer Catacombs

A gnarl of blackberry,
Rose of Sharon and beggar lice

reef a creek hooded with Christ-thorn
and shelves of orange bark-mould

to form the catacombs.
Killdeer wicker and flit

in the briar ceiling
where the light itself is a living thing,

so green it could make you believe
the dead deer will rise to it

on dingy black shoes
and pick up their scattered teeth.

In the peculiar way of their species
they are at once alert and in perfect

repose, the skulls horsy, astonished;
rib cages staving like shipwrecks

out of chartreuse silt,
dead flower-heads in the cavities

nodding on winter stalks; greening
shed racks nibbled by weasels for calcium;

at each skeleton a hide arranged
like a prayer rug.

The Note

I found it in the dew-soaked grass
beneath the apple tree, another bit
of morning trash, along with the fast
food wrappers, cigarette packets,

the inexplicable lone shoe
thrown to our yard in the night.
But this scrap is a note
written on stationary which,

in the lower left corner has
printed the *footprints-in-the-sand poem*—
I don't know what else to call it—
by Margaret Fishback Powers.

Everyone's seen it:
A man dreams he is strolling along
the beach with God,
their footprints side by side.

As his entire life spills out in retrospect,
he notices, however,
that during particularly rough times,
there is only one set of prints.

The man is angry, justifiably so,
it could be argued, and desolate.
Why, he wonders, would the Savior choose
such times to abandon him?

But Jesus, when confronted
with what amounts to betrayal, replies
that when only one set of tracks was visible
it was then, during those bad times,

that he had been carrying the man.
The hand in which the note is written
is careful, perfectly legible,
even practiced, but filled

with elemental spelling and grammar errors:
"I can't take no more,"
"I can't hide this no more,"
"won't take not one thing for what we shared";

"threw" for *through*,
"hole" for *whole*,
"to" for *too*.
What it divulges is minimal.

A woman calling it quits after a three-day fling:
"Am I wrong for loving a married man?"
She mentions a few names I don't recognize.
The signature, though I can make out

"love" and a wry smiley face next to it,
is water-smeared and torn.
It's got to be someone around here.
Our neighbors are sensible,

Christian people.
It is not that they are above adultery;
they simply don't have the stomach for it;
and none I know—

the undertaker, the miller,
the retired prison guard, the dairyman,
their wives—would ever commit
such naked sentiment to paper:

"I love you
more than I have ever loved anyone."
"I hope you get what you want out of life
because I didn't?"

"I'm by myself now and forever."
Who would allow such a document
to float out of her hands?
Since discovering it,

I've kept it on me at all times.
When I sleep I hide it under the Bible
in the top drawer of the nightstand,
my husband sleeping innocently

beside me. Like the woman
in the note, "I am giving it all
up to the Lord,"
<u>Lord</u> underlined twice.

First Day of Fall, Balloon Rally Canceled: Corn

The sigh of torches
gassing hot air balloons

rushes all morning over the corn.
The sky awaits the launch,

the spectrum of aspirating envelopes
champed against the tree bank

still holding what it can of green
fanning clouds marbled with breakwater.

Wind rolls in from the invisible
side of the trees—a land

of gunfire, schizoid dogs and deer.
The balloons, their guy-wires glimmering

in the gattling rain, swoon over yellow ears.
The sky drops its teeth.

There comes a cry from the corn,
torn from its scree soles,

a fortnight till the gleaner,
in lightning taking wing.

The trees utter autumn
and jettison their leaves.

The Stonecarver

This ground makes no pretense at sorrow.
It simply does not remember its dead.
From the firmament Iredell looks like a hatchet
head, precisely hewn of native stone,
sunk in the nape of the Brushies,
its sixteen townships sown with Christians
and those without time to declare.

Mark to my craft my keeping count
of each flake and chisel-cleft that etched
an infant's name in soapstone;
the family, wooled in black,
in its first minute of the mourning year,
tripping back to a wreathed lintel.

Summoned out of Shiloh
I ford roiling Third Creek,
and on hands and knees
in the burnished fallow
reckon the heft of grief,
digging the slave's and pauper's fieldstones,
the freeman's quarried granite,
scratching into them the Golgothan cross,
hopeful verse and the obsessive human need
to record:
Mary, wife of Samuel Harris,
died Oct. 7, 1833
83 y's 8 m's & 17 d's.
As if the lamb rising up
on the third day
had depended on an epitaph.
In the churchyards of Fourth Creek, Bethany,
Snow Creek, Bethesda,
Concord, St. Martin's,

Mount Bethel, Moss Chapel,
junipers rain smoky blue
berries among the nightshade
blooming at the grave collars.
Tolling bellbirds flutter down to feast.

Fitting bit to the ledger stone,
I lift my mallet and write
the endless story of love's pittance
on this wholly indifferent earth.
The Lord's face grizzles with my handiwork.

The Christian Ventriloquist

The ventriloquist's mouth
does not move. His hair
is slick as chrism.
On his lap is a wooden
man with monocle and tuxedo,
red lips, widow's peak,
speedball eyes.
The empty head nods.
The painted jaw clacks:
Jesus this
and Jesus that.

II.

But between what we remember and what really happened are the shadows from which the truth will ultimately reassert itself.

—Peter Ives, "The Whole Truth"

Epigenesis

The moon leavens.
Clumps of petrified potash gleam

like fists in the furrow corrugation.
Gymnosperm spills in the couch grass.

Cropheld and fallow there is more
beneath the sole than upturned by the harrow.

The one pact is earth, its boil and pitch.
Rest against it. Be snatched away.

Listen for fire gouting in the hearths
and tapers of the underhouses,

the Purgatorians chanting Evensong,
spinning dust singlets for their children

seining the Smoke River for bonefish.
Down there the tallow's blue

from the everburn of igneous.
The sky is parchment, the roof you walk upon.

Each dawn, a heart-shaped sun sets it smoldering.
Perhaps the dirt is simply what the field hoards

its grief in, and we must turn away,
ride with all speed from the grave.

But stay the fields, spread your oilskin;
it's all under there:

arrowheads and potsherds, buttons and teeth.
You still love the woman who left out in a gale

from you flat and mumbling on a swith horse to midwife,
left you nothing but the writ's insistence

that there is no death,
left you to chap with the earth.

Do you hear her rising, the rustle
of dirndl, the passel of hungry

little ones mewling in grass blankets?
There where the earth knows to open,

her hair like solstice wheat the day of gleaning,
going grey, but in the moonlight like milkweed

surging out of its pod.
Even the unimagined returns.

Wall at Second Manassas

It attends the moon in secret lean.
Creviced in limestone and granite,

agate and mountain quartz gleam,
a regiment of stone

bordered in buckthorn,
locked against another morning of battle.

Stones not sanctified by whim,
but borne uphill

by patient raging hands.
This need for a wall

comes late in life, vaguely,
with a sense of fear riding night—

much like idolatry,
all in all, a trick

in no way connected to soldiering.
One hundred years

will call its craft contemplation.
Its places will fill with bone.

Forgotten County

A map is a Manichaean tract,
a web of lines and numbers
chiding the spirit
for detaching itself from matter—
nothing so determined as a tar road
boiling through green swamp,
an empty sack of Bulldog Potash,
a man's discarded black boot
raveled in shed snakeskin.

Like the cursor on a Ouija Board,
we divagate the scorched fist of Forgotten.
No bold legend decks it.
Not one "multi-lane highway,"
no points of interest.
Its four towns,
mere eyelets on "hard surface roads,"
boast only the missing.
A jagged blue vein of water writhes
through them, but goes unnamed.

Remorse is the county seat:
senescent, once-lordly houses,
crutched, braced, paint scroffing
like caked rouge on the cheeks of the D.A.R.
In *Deadhand* dozes the ramparts
of a razed Confederate prison.
Hooker: after a Yankee general
or an octoroon whore?

And then dear *Pharoah*:
named for a slave whelped in a tobacco silo
by a tetched white girl
from the county's best family.
Two weeks old

the infant washed up in a hurricane
on the banks of the Pamlico,
trussed by a lynch-knot to a coping stone,
a cross chiseled in his forehead,
and was reincarnated as the town.
You say it couldn't happen?
A dead boy come back as a place?
But I say, map or no, by Bible or bone,
no one knows what makes this land—
nor any other.
For dust to dust, water to water,
and the bastards are dropped in the sea
from whence they return as whole towns.

Forgetfulness lifts an arthritic hand
from each abandoned plow-farm.
In that capitulant swoon of the road,
my family sleeps. Only the kiss
of time will wake them.
Like a lost dog, I stop
and mark my milepost with urine
next to a cornfield gagged
in purple morning glory,
stupefied by drought.
In a brackish ditch, turtles
line a log like an abacus.

The heat takes me to task for being human,
not some creature that can't count past hardship.
Still, I am happy,
happy as I've ever been, racing nightfall
for the vast amnesty of the Atlantic,
poring over my flagging memory
for the little I have known
of the soul's geography,
stumbling about the earth in ignorance.

Bath

The walking tour scuds along Bathtown Commons.
The village sleeps half-sunk

in the Pamlico that has yielded
in the past week of storms

a pregnant doe, and shark with black
boot and grail in its twisted bellows.

Quelled in Calvinist light,
Saint Thomas's and its maze of spiked graves

and jasmine fix the eye of Bath
like a giant forge firing

two blocks of silent houses
along the narrow gabled streets.

Water oaks and magnolias, risen
a thousand years, buckle the cobbles

and wrought pike fences.
This was the hideout of Edward Teach—

a mere ten stone beneath a black beard—
who plundered maidens in his windlass

on the torchlit sound.
His name is carved with the clerics'

in the gunmetal marker
christening the town.

Gulls curl into the churchyard
dipping for oxeye and bloodroot.

The Immaculate Conception

I could scratch a mustache on the woman
modeling lilac butter-fleece
in the *Early Winters* catalogue.

Ridicule:
That would dismiss her, like the Communion
of Saints, from my longing.

Thinsulate acrylic, Merino sheepskin,
hand-knit woolens,
her innocent smile beneath the Roll-rim berber.

Shearling. Like *darling.*
A woman of practical beauty,
long auburn hair coursing out and over

the lintel of her airbrushed photograph
like a holy card;
good with animals and babies,

chaste, yet robust enough to bear fashionably
the Christ-child in an Oregon blizzard,
a helpmate who can build a lasting fire,

wick sweat and even blood from her man
with bare hands, then cook by candlelight.
Even her dog is well-dressed

in ergonomically designed green jacket.
I know better than to fall in love with apparitions.
It is the end of the year, and for now,

my life dulled by imperfection,
I am done with truth.
The world is regret.

All that remains is iconography:
the tall black beautiful hooker
on Trade Street in Charlotte

who squeezed into my Volkswagen
parked in front of First Presbyterian
and offered herself. Today:

the Feast of the Immaculate Conception.
Do you even know what that means?
Behold the Handmaid of the Lord.

Customs

First of the spring primrose ropes
Rue Victoria where the train slows,
grinds through Porte Ste. Jean, then halts

at the New York border for Customs.
The defacement on the wall
of Maison Ethier is in English:

rancid soul. On the Anglican church lawn
squat Burgoyne's fat black cannons.
Golfers in tams and dungarees stroll

the municipal links, towing quivers
of clubs in wheeled caddies. Armed
agents pluck a man from the train,

speak to him in impeccable French.
We glimpse but the back of his head above
the Ginkgo saplings, their young leaves

in the shapes of hearts as he is led across
a field, among great mounds of hay and dung,
a queue of black silos.

The Spirit Homeless

In a field fallow since Stoneman's raid,
a place itself killed and gone to the Master,

if such can be said of land,
they quarter in abandoned automobiles

that seem plunked from space:
snapped axles, wheels slewed

like clubfeet, roofs caved,
windshields busted out with pheasant shot,

sprung doors spilling weedy bedclothes,
crank-case syrup gunked into the quartzy grit.

Freak flowers sprout two-headed, dolt-faced.
Purple-bark elms thrust into the cumulonimbus.

Someone's dump even in the afterlife.
Antique farmcraft froze in rust.

Leaky black barrels of nitrate.
Grain funnels hove beast-like in extremis.

Possums die in their sleep,
turn cipher-black,

whiptailed to thorny locust beams.
A deer stand hulks like a time machine.

These folks are forgot, nothing but lot
numbers in a grown-over churchyard.

Still they transmigrate back
to make the better of travail.

In spirit coitus they renew the shadow world.
Babies in dirt cratches teethe on bone and cordite.

So same-feeling this wandering
hand-to-mouth grubbing,

they reckon it's flesh and blood all over again,
a new batch of dog-tired. Not deceasement,

that one last give-out
where you swap denim and feedcloth

for a second-hand glory robe, scrubbed to shimmering
threadbare, and a serviceable crown.

Habit is a cross.
Be anxious for nothing.

All a body need do is cry out for forgiveness.
They muddle about their business,

slopping supper pans in Scotts Creek,
gnawing on dried hackberries,

mucking through honey boxes
ringwormed with petrified combs,

tending fire, crafting whiskey of compost.
They have mislaid the particulars of their exile:

this ever coming back, this ever remaining
cumbered in the wilderness to make amends,

scratching naked through the woods
for that one pigtrot into the kingdom.

White Lake, Bladen County

At the verge of White Lake,
I lean against a pier stob and stare

at stars raked over the Bladen sky.
A sun-murdered sandbar

boasting the continent's oldest Magnolia,
this string of lakes, spring-fed.

Not even a boat ripple
this time of night—

only the gurgle of phantoms
at its rim slipping in like lovers

at moonless midnight, the water
invisible, crystalline, the shore

a makeshift of silent lights fizzing
from cheap getaway thatches.

At the Silver Sands, my family
waits for me in our kitchenette

where we'll fall asleep
in front of an unfamiliar TV.

I wonder who we are. But the water
does not wonder. Nor the sky,

nor the stars, nor the half-trees
sunk in the shallows,

wearing in their fracted branches
wings of Spanish moss.

Off South Carolina 9 in Little Rock

In a dogleg off South Carolina 9
in Little Rock reigns
the Victorian church of Saint Paul.

Its homage to Methodism
has baked on its flaking walls
and listing graveyard obelisks

for two hundred years.
It has seen drought before, and faith
hamstrung by dirt and water.

All that grow and go unfamished
are the sweating bone orchards.
Legions of sunflowers lift brazen faces

to the cruel white sun amok
among lynched corn. Shucks
hang brown and flayed

from tasseled hags near silking,
pilling from split maws
eth. Dead chickens

cks to the landfill.
ot swing their heavy heads
e sea traffic,

d;
l cudless.
on barrels,

stare into their hats, in the yard
of a boarded-up auction barn
and wait for hay from Illinois.

Jackdaws dance on carcasses in the road.
The yellow line burns itself
clear to Horry County

where the continent ends
in the clutches of brine.
From the broken lintel

of her drawn-up house, a woman
holds a baby and gapes
at the sealed red doors of the church.

Rendition

Getting to the old Anson house by wagon
on the gullied two-track gripped in bled corn
bottoms us into a sawgrass sump.
From there we walk, praying
it's turned off too cold for the moccasins
that rope the river shelf.

"You were whelped here," I tell the boy.
In one foxed corner of his dream life
he remembers from an infant's fancy
the house, a hundred years haunted
by barrenness before he arrived.

When he was born the black croppers
from Lilesville came like thurifers
spreading beneath the house snake sulphur,
the color of sun and bad-milk-smelling
to run off the mating vipers.
They thought the little white baby
was Jesus come
to resurrect the corn.

This too I tell him.
He doesn't quite fathom it, though
he knows it's a story—
like his birth home
we trample on toward in the dark—
a rendition of the way things may have been.

From a distance it looks the same,
but we smell what's left of it:
shrunken by fire, the arsonist's flight,
three days' rain and the night
wall at its throat.

I enter alone.
Black stalactites devil the ceiling.
Planks still sweat from the match.
Night smears the gash in the roof
where the chimney bricks crashed.
At the poker table in the library
scorched haints hunker
in coveralls of smoke,
clutching in their fingers,
black as cheroots,
charred suits of spades and hearts.
From the shelves, words spill
like coals out of books.
The Bible is carbon.
The jackpot smolders
like the memory of the night
I laid at the hearth
with the boy's mother and took fire.

My son waits for me in the spot
where I used to stand with the moon
on my head, wondering
what he might be pondering in the womb.
He watches deer sweep
over the swales to Savannah Creek.
"We can fix it up and come back," he says.
In the woods, torchlight flickers.
A wildcat screams.
"Yes," I answer.

John

Because I have loved this woodchuck,
marked at the shoulder his wistful matins,
paws grinding together at his breast
like beads as he gazed out of the brown hood

of his fur at the Brushies.
I crave the instinct
upon which his mind fastened
when into his eyes bore the distant plateau,

his insideness as he slid back
at my passing into his cope.
John, my son and I named him,
conjured stories to construe

our parts in his woodchuck's life.
We gave him family, house, a job.
Auction signs post along Scotts Creek,
old homesteads smashed

and carried off in trucks.
The seared dirt sprouts surveyors' spikes.
My son loses his baby teeth.
"No, that is not John," I insist

when we see on the road crown
the hump of sodden fur and heart
spilt on the double yellow.
John's teeth score into the asphalt.

Buzzards drape the trees.
I am close enough to see
their thrumming wattles
as they hawk up carrion.

Copperheads, I've been told,
are mating with black snakes—
out there
where engines click through the woods.

After dark, I slide my hand
under my son's pillow
and feel for his tooth.
Loosed from him,

it is a thing of other-ken,
wild, belonging to no one.
In its place I leave silver.
We'll never tell good from bad again.

Something From A Book

(For Jacob)

He'd rather read than anything.
Even in his sleep we find him

cradling a book, his place marked
with his prayer-locked hands,

the words like tracks across the stripped
pelagic cornfields he roams in his sleep.

The roots, appending from the foot-high cane,
look in the blue moon dawn

like baby fingers up to the knuckles
in loam. I find him slaloming among

the stalks, waving his book, twinkling
like brilliantine in the dew-bloody

sun, red, winning sky inch
by inch. He is outside me,

cinematic, farther than my call.
As if from a fable, geese, moaning,

lunge out of the brake he sleepwalks;
and I am sure they will pluck him

from this misdoubtful world, lift
him as they might a charmed prince.

But instead they beat about him a wind
that carries them into the sun and my son

into them, the pages of his book
ungumming, then whirling, his hair

like feathers blown about his still
sleeping head—like something from a book.

Holy Week

Monday:
Simon knuckles along the rivermost curve,
tailing the share, toting dawn sun
like shield and buckler, dropping
seeds from a purple rag, furrow
and plow-sole an inch from his startled eye.
Creek and Pee Dee arrowheads,
black bones, furzy blue dung of predators,
a doe chasing a black dog.
Nor does he resist his ear:
the addled stuttering of Lazarus;
Isaias, six days before
Passover; the pegleg shade
whose roods he sows as did his daddy
(the ghost's chauffer and plowboy),
outliver of hoodoo and sortilege
in the valley of madmen and plucked girls.
There beneath the hawk, torn
on the wing by crows,
the tilled voices sign and bicker.
The one-eyed mule goes loco,
splits its hames and traces.
Iscariot sulks.
Jesus screams.
Simon on his knees,
hat in the parched clay,
eyes clamped, ears plugged.
Sundown.

Tuesday:
Deer climb from the gravel pit,
white tails flashing: six, then one
cut from the herd by the black dog,

disappearing into the swamp.
Simon turns four circles;
spits north, south, east and west;
studies his good black book:
I shall strangle the rooster,
tack horseshoes o'er my pallet
and no ghost shall enter my domicile
to drink my wine and foul my grapes.
I shall strike from the soil
thistle, buckthorn and chokecherry,
mock orange and locust, rose,
blackberry, burdock and cockleburr.
I shall load my flintlock and twelve
gauge and sport my daddy's fedora
plaited with peach blossoms
and lilies of the valley;
and shall not be the object of Anglo wagers
nor the butt of their drunken anthems.

Wednesday:
Dreaming of moonshine and murder,
the ploughshare's rancor,
a brown man on a tree,
hemp oozing blood and pitch,
he sleeps on flintlock and wattled lucre
stuffed in the sand and sawdust mattress.
Purple sun sluices through pine and yellow
clouds of pollen. Fawns rise
out of new grass like dyed garments.
Martins eaten by snakes as they couple.
Horseflies and bluebottles idle and bang
the sorry walls of Simon's shack.
The mob in his head builds a necropolis.
He wakes laughing—shotguns in the swamp—
surrounded by his brothers of grave

and madcap litany:
Jesus of the sawmill,
gravel pit and factory;
Confederate Jesus, indentured, white trash;
Chaingang Jesus;
Good Shepherd, bad, sorry, redbone, jackanape;
Shotgun Jesus;
Food stamp Jesus, face-hiding, jacklegged;
Low-stone Jesus, breaking bad;
Blind Jesus, lame;
The Sacred Heart, the safest heart;
Infant of Anson, naked, motherless,
terrified, daddyless,
inbred, androgynous, slave;
Sundown Jesus;
Moonrise Jesus;
Amen Jesus.

Thursday:
Possums swell at the shoulder—
teeth and empty sockets. Gobbling crows.
Simon sucks a poorboy of sticky pink wine.
His eyes cloud over bean can and white ham,
cane and poke salad, wood for bread.
At his boots, the dead rooster—
strangled meat. Falls out drunken,
plucking, dreams: *He is called*
to pastoring. His face is rock
that cracks the hands of strikers.
Lost dogs wander the long, littered road
of smashed carapace and silent fur,
tar and black bone, old voices.
Sherman's dragoons torch the woods.
His daddy dragged behind a mule,
Mama's dress bloodied.

He washes the feet of runaway slaves.
Live deer burn across the fields.
Flaming hawks plummet from buckling pines.
Air filled with earth and spinning balls.
The pegleg ghost rides a mammoth black stallion.
Tallow-mouthed, Simon wakes,
clawing at his mother's Bible,
buzzards knifed on a lunate moon
hanging in the dead Judas.

Friday:
By jug and haunch Simon, vested
in dirt, climbs the hickory and sits nattering
like a starling on the lone transverse beam,
switching himself senseless.
Lightning flogs the orchard.
Peach blossoms explode.
The horse takes the wire at a gallop,
goes down splintered in the ditch,
barbs braided cross his flanks and withers.
Brown ghosts, waving lynched fists,
scrip and bale-tallies, sprout from loam
of spike and noose; go forth
to hammer on the red doors of the missions
and settle with the alchemistical
preachers and ferret-faced gospel drummers,
razing shack and shanty, weeping, praising:
"Not a bone of him shall you break."

Saturday:
In the privy at sunrise,
hunched over dregs of shothouse vespers,
he dreams of cottoned headlands,
alabaster and arrowroot,
the pigment of saints and politicians.

Staggers down to the blazed and flaking stones,
the glad rotting hush where someone
in the long ago hankered after love and mercy,
and chipped the words into rock beneath
the vanished names which knew neither
and were blown away as dust.
Simon tastes the words in his mouth.
They choke and burn him like a scorched boll.
He cocks the flintlock,
licks the worn stock, slides
the rusty barrel down his throat.
An old voice concurs.
A train whistle reckons salvation.

Sunday:
Wakes to blackberry winter,
fits feet to earth, strips and washes
in the chapel stream; looking up
spies the giant buck with swirling
rack among the burnished markers.
In its ancient eye before it bolts
he sights himself alive; and the words,
at first hot on his tongue, yet slowly cooling,
return to Simon—the sudden almsman
shivering in the surcease of flame.
He falls on the graves, throttling them,
begging the millstone grit
in which the soul of his ancestry sleeps
for love and mercy.
Selah.

Julian

... in cases of necessity any person may baptize ...
— *The Catholic Catechism*

In christening gown and bonnet,
he is white and stoic as the moon,
unflinching as the sun burns
through yellow puffs of pine
pollen gathered at his crown
while I pour onto his forehead
from a tiny blue Chinese rice cup
holy water blessed

by John Paul II himself
and say, "I baptize you, Julian Joseph,
in the name of the Father, and of the Son,
and of the Holy Spirit."
Nor does he stir when the monarchs
and swallowtails,
in ecclesiastical vestments,
lift from the purple brushes
of the butterfly bush
and light upon him.

Drought

(For Beckett)

A batting slump leaguers my six year old.
Balls from his bat which rung
off our tin roof nest
in the brown, withered June grass,
wild onions the only tenuous green
between the sun and the water table,
sixteen inches to the bad and falling,
scarecrow farmers maundering
among clicking kernels of dead wheat.

Strike after futile strike,
he implores I pitch when it is obvious
it will have to come back on its own.
Like Elias, summoning rain, he flails,
the 27-inch silver Adirondack
like a wroth prophet's sword,
until he can no longer lift his arms;
parsing through the neurotic tics
of the hexed hitter:
adjusting his stance, swapping bats,
crossing himself, pawing
with his bare toes at the cracked earth.

Long past dusk, the ball graying
in the falling night,
after I have gone in to draw his rationed bath,
he drills, fearful
that hitting, like God, is simply random:
one day a blessing, the next a curse.

From an open cookbook he learns Babe Ruth
ate scallions to cure slumps.
There is a caricature of the Bambino
in pinstripes swinging a giant scallion
in the on-deck circle.
I explain they are onions, which he abhors,
from the lily family,
that the Egyptians believed
they symbolized the world.

His first bite leaves him paralyzed,
catatonic, the dusty face beneath the hat-bill
suddenly old and drained.
Each meal he eats them,
tears washing his cheeks as he gnashes,
then out to the yard.
Still no rain,
the waxing moon so bright it is a sound,
lording above the grizzled ground
off which he grazes like a baby
satyr on wild onions.

The night of the solstice
I hear from my bed the telltale thunder
of a ball launched off a bat
an instant before rain pellets
down on the roof, then
the relentless *whoosh* as water
resounds in endless ovation. Slowly,
the land, upon which my cured son stands,
opens, so very very slowly,
to the sky, at last,
its sealed lips.

The Cartographer

"Memory is genius, really."
—Robert Lowell

While she was gone he left
with his arsenal of maps and watched

the house through a grove of motley cedars.
No wind. Still heat.

Smoke from his cigarette spiraled up,
reminding him of the ibises

wading in the Jumna River,
years ago, in Uttar Pradesh.

He spat into the air.
Real mosquitoes, those.

At day's end, he'd comb hundreds
from his hair and beard.

She could sit pretty among them and never flinch.
It had been lovely to watch her,

as he did now as she swept aside
the curtains to allow in the morning sun.

There was more to it than that.
But he had memory for nothing else.

The mosquitoes enraged him.
He could kill only two; the second,

fat with blood, stained his shirt.
His hands swarmed his body as if

all he wanted was to be touched.
The woman entered the yard

and began gathering leaves.
He thought of the Himalayas,

knelt and put his ear to earth,
twice bolted up and didn't breathe.

He could recall a day like this with her,
but could not quite make the connection.

III.

And in any event, I know now that the whole truth of anything is an idea that stops existing finally.

—Richard Ford, "Great Falls"

Mysterium Tremendum

In Greenville, North Carolina,
I leave my hotel room, its witness

of anonymity—telephone, remote,
microwave, pristine glossy Gideon

secreted in the nightstand like a straight razor—
accept the evening's invitation,

its cool dark hand in mine,
the lascivious flicker of its middle finger

against my palm, and cross
the neon boulevard for coffee.

In line, ahead of me, just one guy,
tall, ascetic, cowled in red and black

Atlanta Falcons hoody, the angry bird of prey
jessed to his back like a hex sign.

He orders two apple pies, hands the clerk,
in pin stripes and Wyatt Earp tie, a five.

When she opens the drawer for change,
he strikes across the counter,

swoops up the green bills,
those eluding him fluttering

in the updraft, rows of cups and cutlery
behind the woozy clerk toppling:

the slow silent filmic tumult of a miracle
as the robber, a kid,

beautiful as a Trappist acolyte,
slices out the door, hops a rickety

bicycle, pedals tiptoe, clawed up
by that regal bird on his back

into the forgetful mysterium
of night, sirens already heralding

his shrouded arrival,
his glorious departure.

Advising

The woman I advise tests
into Remedial. I explain
the courses she must take before
she actually accrues college credit.

We both refer to them as *brush-up*.
She works a 10 to 6 a.m. shift
at the Sara Lee factory
forty miles east in the next county.

Her plan is to clock out,
come to school for a couple hours
each morning, then go home and sleep
before it all starts up again.

The boy with her is named Jason.
He throws a yellow ball,
then trips after it.
"Just turned three in October,"

she corrects me when I guess too high at his age.
Tall and handsome, orangish hair
curling around his caramel face.
Pacifier. Dallas Cowboys sweats.

Swelling out of the little desk,
the woman's distracted, big, blonde;
her skin, factory white;
nothing to write with, so I give

her my pen and guide her
through the Federal Funding questionnaire:
AFDC, JTPA, VA, VR, GED,
various impairments, disabilities ...

Jason chases the ball about the classroom.
"C'mere," she says repeatedly,
though he pays no attention.
Then he wheels and whips the ball at me.

I try to catch it, but it hits me
instead in the chest.
"You're a bad boy, Jason," she barks.
"That man's going to get you."

The boy looks at me.
His eyes are blue.
"He's not a bad boy," I say.
"You want him?" she shoots back.

Jason stares at me,
spit dribbling off the end of the pacifier.
"Yes," I answer.
"I'm going to go on and leave you

here with this man," she scolds.
Before I can say another word,
the boy starts crying.
His face fills with water, the nipple

of the dripping pacifier visible
as he opens his mouth to catch his breath.
She hoists him onto her desktop
and he begins to hush, heaving

every few seconds, holding onto her T-shirt.
Where's your ball?" she asks.
Then to me: "I'm crazy. Ain't I?"
I smile, but can't think of the thing to say.

I tell her to sign above my signature,
then direct her to the Registrar's office
where she'll have to pay.
She slides the baby to her.

As she lifts him and rises,
I see that his pants are sopping.
He leaves a trail of wet along the formica.
"Bye, Jason," I call;

but he seems asleep,
his ball still sitting in my lap,
his urine on the desktop
catching light from the window.

Pumpkins

Ninety days ago
in summer's forge,

the pumpkin farmer fingered
into each little mound

four face-shaped seeds that vaunt
into cropness after three days under.

There is not much for it,
but to pray for rain and kindness

against parasites. Each day
the vines, like umbilici, threaten

not to live, to draw back into
the omphalos, refusing to yield

the yellow vulviform blossoms
that pine against wet black loam.

Best before the first fruit
to pluck and eat the flowers.

Once they blush, there is only
salt and cedar ash to dose them

and drive back the swarm of purple glories.
But in the end

squash bugs like sin gnawing
from within out corrupt them.

They sore, then suppurate.
No one will look at them

nor carve into their flesh at harvest
faces of fire.

Design

Between before and after is the narrow passage,
so deliberate in its suddenness as to be unlikely.

It is part of a plan that blocks the scene so carefully
that the child and the snake become for each other

shapes of color: the child in motley, proof
against hunters; and the snake, a timber rattler,

curled like a turban in a sun-patch not molten,
but the merest brown, its tail a bracelet

of wooden snap beads. Only after the child
sets his boot a millimeter from its mouth and lifts it

to jump the creek and scramble up the far bank,
the snake lunges like a sword from its pile,

an expression of nothingness on its face,
then disappears quietly into the leaves.

The Sorrow of Forgetting

What would you, holy maiden
Of that rock face, cold and grim?
Were you seeking for a loved one
When you knelt in prayer to Him?
              —"The Kneeling Nun"
              —Lou Curtis Foster

The streets of sabbath Albuquerque
are abandoned. I walk
Route 66, the Mother Road,
through the marrow of town,
stop for a moment to look at suits
of armor in an antique shop window.
A boy and girl appear.
She clutches the dangling hand
of the arm he's draped over her shoulder.
In her cropped copper hair bud
pink Tamarisk clusters.
I want to catch their eyes,
but they walk by, laughing,
as if I'm not there.

Outside the station, an Isleta woman
sells silver and turquoise.
I buy a pair of earrings for my wife—
tiny pueblo rock houses—and write
to her back in the unfathomable
green east of Appalachia.
A postcard in the center of which
is a *66* enclosed by the U.S. Highway
symbol that looks so much like a heart
sliced in half by I-25 to Santa Fe.
I tell her I'm in Albuquerque,
boarding the train for the badlands,
then on to California.
I tell her I guess that's all there is to say.

Somewhere out there in the blinding gypsum
lay Flower Mountain, Ambrosia Lake,
jackpile mines and yellowcake,
the petrified stumps of Navajo
peach trees slaughtered by Kit Carson.
Along the railhead slums
of the uranium belt, secreted once beneath
blue water, the crumbling churches
of New Mexico lance over pueblos
blistered Spanish crosses.

I'm tempted to think of train travel
as sad. But, as I settle into my berth,
and the earth's brute majesty
streams across my eyes,
I spy a doddering old horse
wandering a narrow canyon
of saguaro and mesquite;
and I realize it's amnesia,
the great sorrow of forgetting,
that afflicts us all.

On a far rise looms an altar-like mesa
and, upon it, a black volcanic monolith
natives call The Kneeling Nun.
Long ago, a beautiful sister
fled the convent for love
of a wounded soldier
she miraculously healed,
then ventured with him
into the forbidden world.
Yet after a time she longed
to return to her vows.
But her transgressions were unforgivable.
God turned her to stone.

Peaches

On a roadhouse bathroom wall
in the peach town of Gaffney, South Carolina,
a woman's body laminates itself
across the face of a condom machine,
her legs spread to accommodate the notched
silver knob one turns after
fitting four bits in the slot.

Not quite naked,
her lips pout crimson,
long dark hair obscuring breasts that sink
slowly into a loose black camisole,
hands writhing in a cat's cradle
at her G-string.

They come in a full spectrum of color:
Classic, French Tickler, Lubricated,
Extra-strength, Ultra-thin, Reservoir-tip,
Vibra-ribbed, the Pleasure Ring.
"Don't look at that," I command my transfixed sons;
and they turn away at the very instant
they would have been struck to salt or blinded.

The three of us use the lone toilet,
cigarettes floating in the yellow brine.
The boys, mugging at the smell, aim for the butts.
"Don't touch a thing," I bark,
lifting my boot to the flush-handle.
Then we soap and wash and wash again,
the Goddess of Hygiene staring down upon us
as they towel their hands on my jeans.

Back on the road, peach trees
come at us from all sides,
somehow cruel in winter,
sharpened like tenterhooks
clawing at the dripping horizon.
In the center of the vast orchards,
rising monolithic on its four storey golf tee,
sprouts a water tower
designed as a giant peach, roseate,
luscious and long, its flange
suggesting perfectly the buttocks
of a voluptuous woman
bent slightly forward.

"What is a condom?" asks my older son.
"For birth control," I answer.
He makes a guttural sound, signaling his disgust;
yet boys come to condoms
in startlingly original ways.
I find myself looking at my wife,
gazing out the passenger window
at the scrum of trees waiting for spring
to bear on their naked twigs
pink flowers.

House-Hunting at Four Thousand Feet

The road's not but a ledge,
near straight up, shale
and millstone. Mud.
Good God, come winter.
Three slough-bellied brown
and white bangtail paints cleat
to a shelf in the mist,
then a bouquet of pink plastic roses
stabbed in the scarp ahead of the fall-off.
By the time we find the house,
fog's set in and we can't see to turn around.
Shear on both sides.
The children wear those silent worried looks.
They don't want to live in the sky
where a thing mishandled plummets
the better part of a mile;
and all there is for it is to cock an ear
and reckon altitude by the *whump*.
Pray each time your foot touches earth.
Hold on like Hades.
Folks up here are born cloven and slouch.
Purchase is bred well-deep into them.
The house is slant, lank,
with enough give to weather gravity,
and thus plumb.
Appalachian physics.
We creep up and beam the brights on it.
It eyes right back, querulous
like a bedridden crone, but old man too,
finicky, the tin roof
a rusted skullcap.
Thick watery glass windows,
cataracted with silica,

yellow dauber nests
like sleep mortised into the panes.
Up here is odd enough to make a house
not just thingful, but a someone
with blood and breath. Secrets.
Voices. Some say
you get used to it:
catamounts, fog, rime-ice,
the wind like Deuteronomy
when it gets het up,
snow beading down,
shrinking everything in its alabaster clout.
We venture no farther than the spinney
gnarling the busted porch,
demur like the beholden Israelites
and wait for a sign, our eyes
discomfited by everlasting up.

The Vilas Flood

From the outset, the wind
signals the water's rise,
its sudden inflorescence
stitched across the meadow,

trout heaving on the swill, speckled,
mortis-eyed. Crows: black
ingots on the green-gray gout.
Goldfinches drown in mid-flight.

Swallowtails sucked off in the spindrift.
Look out and it's a downpour.
Glance again and it's a river licking
at the porch, Crawfords' house

about took, Jacky's trailer under,
sun burning up there in the calamity
bright yellow—some diluvial hex.
What rolls out of the gap cross-lashes

the bridge spanning the gorged stream—
fenders of water, six, eight feet high—
detonating it. A red geyser spouts
from the plank flinders and sprung sandbags

as though the cork capping Purgatory
gassed out. Linville Creek,
a dark glistening documentary
of outlandish migration flashes

through the flume, on its back
the archaeology of Vilas.
Isaac's bawling calf, split tether snaked
in the roil, rushes by.

As if spirited out of the tallow,
coyotes, smoky whisps of bony pelt,
mince on the oozing bank,
paw and snap, weep and coo

as the baby angus disappears.
Then an entire apple tree
loaded with red winesaps.
Buckeyes still ivory asleep

in their green sarcophagi.
A pumphouse. A gazebo
and a wagon tongue.
Cord upon cord of split wood.

Then the coolers and tools and baby dolls.
Kayak paddles. A Lousiville Slugger
signed by Rocky Colavito.
A white leatherbound Bible,

its writ in Spanish. Whatever
might dislodge from largesse
and parsimony. The grand.
The infinitesimal. All left to rot

and propagate, finally forgotten,
as far downstream as Zionville.
Even the wedding gown draped
like a jilted bride over a haybale.

Running

(For Leon)

I recite the rosary
Hail Mary when I run,
a wooden bead *full of grace*
per so many meters: for the winter wheat,
coy *blessed* barely green beneath
the purple *art thou* Lenten crown vetch;
the sun that rations color *among women and blessed*
sitting in its cupboard ripening
like a pomegranate *is the fruit*;
the frayed, porous moon *of thy womb*
dissolving on the tongue
of blue morning *Jesus*;
cows, musk of their bowels
scenting the fog, still as tintypes;
deer *Holy Mary* gazing skyward in wonder
at the cry of Canada geese;
papery corn shucks whispering at my feet;
strips of loose tin from an infolded barn
thundering in the wind-lash;
my print *Mother of God*
alongside the raccoon's and skunk's
as I leap the creek bed
and cross Stikeleather land,
posted black letters on yellow handbills
tacked to the shaven thighs of Sycamores;
chicken houses a mile off
on Midway Road whitening in the now-
lightening horizon *pray*;
and far beyond in Alexander County,
on looming Fox Mountain, nectarines
that will hold migrants hostage
all spring flower.

I gulp another quart of ether,
dig *for us sinners*
up the steep farm road to intercept
the risen sun, sprint the crest,
my chest filled with pink shrapnel,
and fall into it,
a stretched and sweating shadowgraph.
For this searing instant
one chases *now and at the hour*
in the darkness every morning
the improbability *of our death*
that legs with hearts to prompt them
may keep lurching, decade upon decade,
chaplet upon chaplet, toward salvation *Amen.*

JOSEPH BATHANTI was born and raised in Pittsburgh, PA. He came to North Carolina as a VISTA Volunteer in 1976 to work with prison inmates. Bathanti is the author of four books of poetry: *Communion Partners; Anson County; The Feast of All Saints;* and *This Metal,* which was nominated for The National Book Award. His first novel, *East Liberty,* winner of the Carolina Novel Award, was published in 2001. His latest novel, *Coventry,* won the 2006 Novello Literary Award. *They Changed the State: The Legacy of North Carolina's Visiting Artists, 1971-1995,* his book of nonfiction, was published in early 2007. Most recently, his collection of short stories, *The High Heart,* winner of the 2006 Spokane Prize, was published by Eastern Washington University Press in 2007. He is the recipient of a Literature Fellowship from the North Carolina Arts Council; The Samuel Talmadge Ragan Award, presented annually for outstanding contributions to the Fine Arts of North Carolina over an extended period; the Linda Flowers Prize; the Sherwood Anderson Award, the 2007 Barbara Mandigo Kelly Peace Poetry Prize; and others. He is Professor of Creative Writing at Appalachian State University in Boone, NC.

Printed in the United States
212017BV00001B/2/P

9 780981 628073